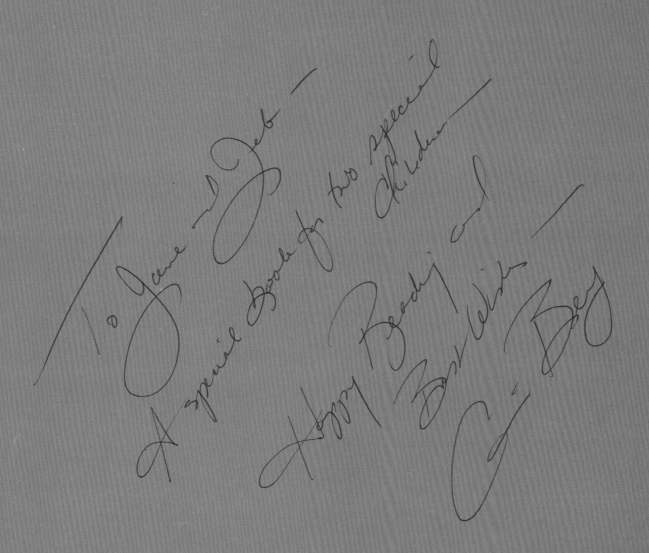

To Jamie and Deb —
A special book for two special children —

Happy Reading and
Best Wishes —

Cris Berg

ILLUSTRATED
BY JANET BIONDI

TEXT
BY CAMI BERG

WINDOM BOOKS

D

IS
FOR

DOLPHIN

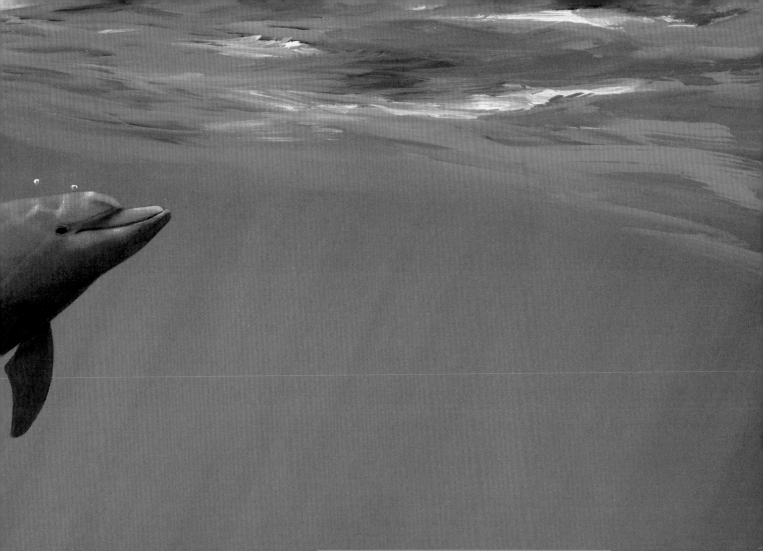

A

IS

FOR

AIR

B

IS

FOR

BLOWHOLE

C

IS

FOR

CALF

D

IS

FOR

DIVING

E

IS

FOR

EYE

F
IS
FOR
FLIPPERS

G IS FOR GRACEFUL

H

IS

FOR

HUNGRY

I

IS

FOR

INHALATION

J

IS

FOR

JUMPING

K

IS

FOR

KINDNESS

L

IS

FOR

LANGUAGE

M

IS

FOR

MAMMAL

N

IS

FOR

NURSING

O

IS

FOR

OCEAN

P

IS

FOR

POD

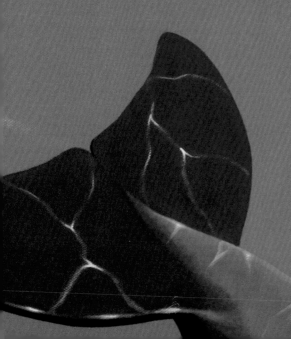

Q

IS

FOR

QUICK

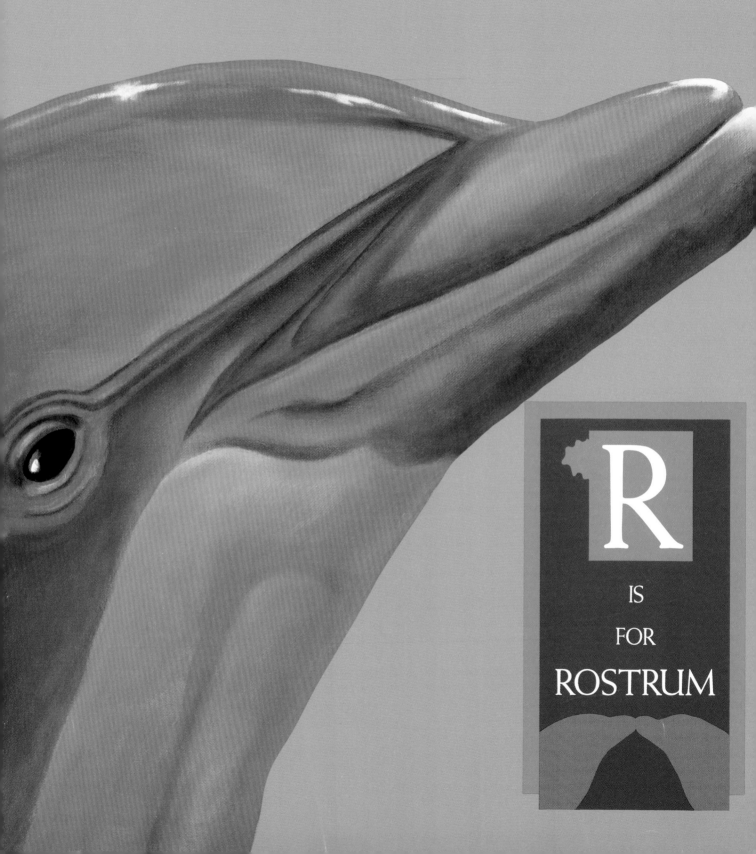

R

IS

FOR

ROSTRUM

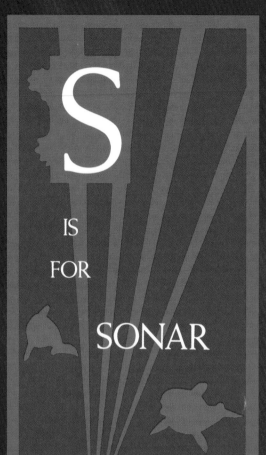

S

IS

FOR

SONAR

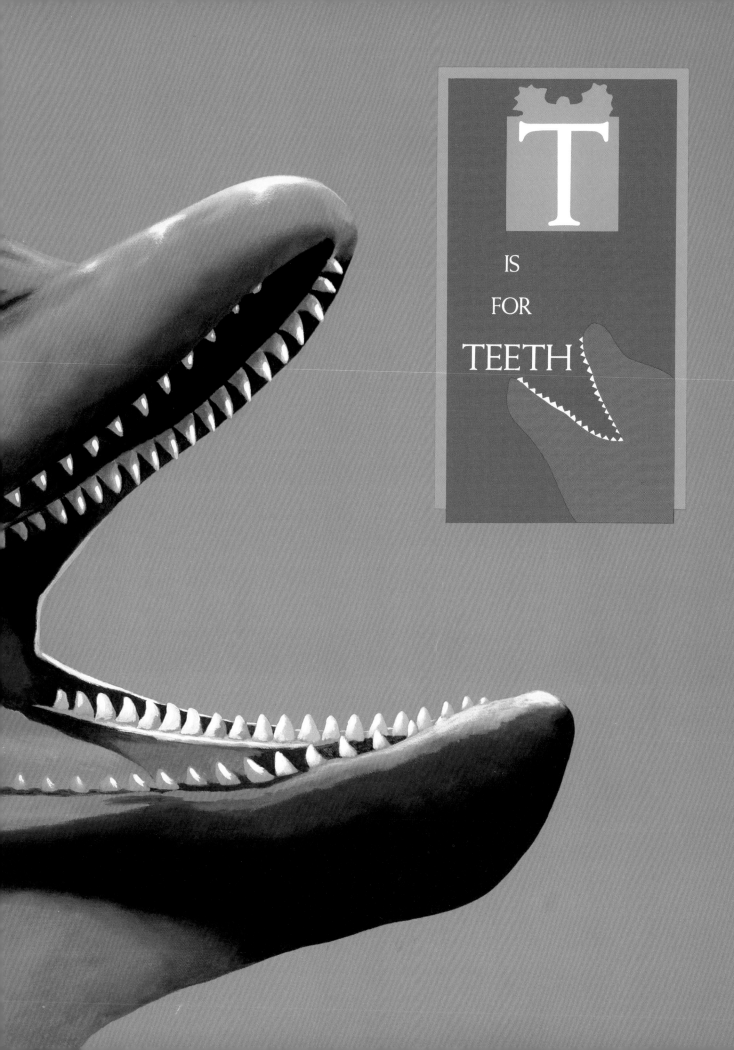

T

IS

FOR

TEETH

U

IS

FOR

UPSIDE

DOWN

V

IS

FOR

VERTICAL

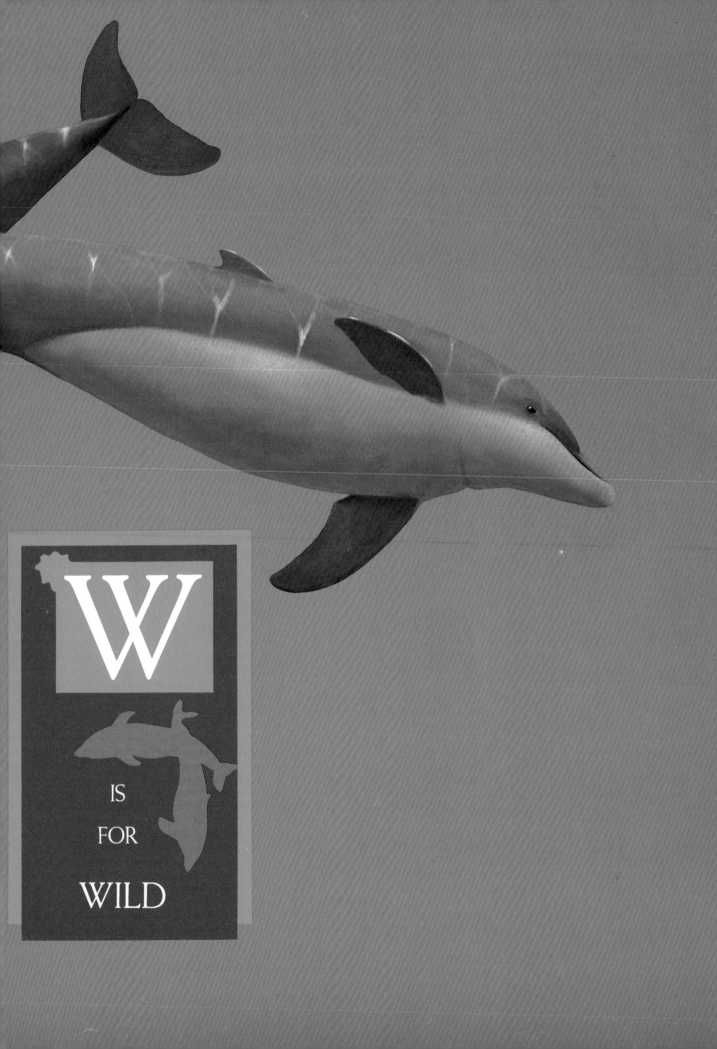

W

IS

FOR

WILD

X

IS

FOR

eXCEPTIONAL

Y

IS

FOR

YEARNING

Z

IS

FOR

ZZZzz

A   All dolphins breathe air.

B   A dolphin breathes through his or her blowhole, a curved opening at the top of the head.

C   Immediately after a baby dolphin (a calf) is born, the mother guides the calf up to the air.

D   Dolphins love to dive deep.

E   Dolphins can see with their eyes and also with their sonar. Just past each eye is a tiny hole,—the ear.

F   With the help of flippers, a dolphin steers through the ocean. Each flipper has 5 finger-like bones.

G   Gracefulness comes naturally to these 400 pound animals.

H   Dolphins eat fish. They like mackerel, squid, and mullet.

I Although dolphins can hold their breath underwater for 10 minutes, they usually rise to the surface to breathe once or twice every minute.

J Jumping and playing are favorite dolphin activities.

K An injured dolphin often is raised to the ocean surface by other dolphins. Dolphins will also rescue a drowning person.

L Dolphins communicate with clicks, beeps, and whistles and in other languages unknown to humans.

M Dolphins are mammals. Mother dolphins give birth to calves who are born tail first.

N A calf feeds on its mother's milk during the first year of its life.

O The ocean is the dolphin's home. Please keep the ocean clean.

P A family of dolphins is called a pod.

Q Dolphins can swim 25 miles per hour or more. One flip of their flukes, and they are out of sight.

R The rostrum is the dolphin's snout.

W Dolphins are wild animals. They belong in the wild.

S Using their sonar, dolphins are able to find one another in the ocean.

X Dolphins are exceptional beings whose brains are larger than human brains.

T A dolphin has more than 100 teeth. These teeth are used only to catch fish.

Y Captive dolphins yearn for the open ocean.

U Dolphins can swim upside down.

V Sometimes they hang vertically in the water.

Z Ocean dolphins sleep by floating tail down at the top of the ocean. They sleep with their eyes open and only for a few minutes at a time.

To Windham & Tiana
with love,
Janet

Many thanks to Ric O'Barry, Steve McCulloch,
and Ron Canning. And to all dolphins, free and
captive, many thanks for your unending
inspiration and patience with mankind.

A flip of the fluke
and special thanks to
Bonnie, Burt, Ruth and Russell,
Gil, Bill, and Margaret

c.b.

Illustrations copyright © 1991 by Janet Biondi
Text copyright © 1991 by Cami Berg
Text design © 1991 by GLYPHICS

Designed by
GLYPHICS/Terry Duffy Design

ISBN #1-879244-01-2

First Edition
Printed in the USA